A Note to Parents

DK READERS is a compelling prog
designed in conjunction with leadin
Dr. Linda Gambrell, Distinguished P
Clemson University. Dr. Gambrell h̶a̶   …̶resident of
the National Reading Conference, the College Reading
Association, and the International Reading Association.

Beautiful illustrations and superb full-color photographs
combine with engaging, easy-to-read stories to offer a fresh
approach to each subject in the series. Each DK READER is
guaranteed to capture a child's interest while developing his
or her reading skills, general knowledge, and love of reading.

The five levels of DK READERS are aimed at different
reading abilities, enabling you to choose the books that are
exactly right for your child:

Pre-level 1: Learning to read
Level 1: Beginning to read
Level 2: Beginning to read alone
Level 3: Reading alone
Level 4: Proficient readers

The "normal" age at which a child begins to read
can be anywhere from three to eight years old.
Adult participation through
the lower levels is very helpful
for providing encouragement,
discussing storylines, and
sounding out unfamiliar words.

No matter which level you
select, you can be sure that
you are helping your child learn
to read, then read to learn!

LONDON, NEW YORK, MUNICH,
MELBOURNE, AND DELHI

Series Editor Deborah lock
US Senior Editor Shannon Beatty
Project Art Editor Hoa Luc
Producers, Pre-production Francesca Wardell,
Vikki Nousiainen
Illustrator Tim McDonagh

Reading Consultant
Linda Gambrell, Ph.D.

DK DELHI
Editor Pomona Zaheer
Assistant Art Editor Yamini Panwar
DTP Designers Anita Yadav, Vijay Khandwal
Picture Researcher Sumedha Chopra
Deputy Managing Editor Soma B. Chowdhury

First American Edition, 2014
Published in the United States by DK Publishing
345 Hudson Street, New York, New York 10014

14 15 16 17 10 9 8 7 6 5 4 3 2 1
001–256582–June/2014

A catalog record for this book is available
from the Library of Congress.

ISBN: 978-1-4654-2007-7 (Paperback)
ISBN: 978-1-4654-2006-0 (Hardcover)

DK books are available at special discounts when purchased in bulk for
sales promotions, premiums, fund-raising, or educational use.
For details, contact:
DK Publishing Special Markets
345 Hudson Street, New York, New York 10014
SpecialSales@dk.com

Printed and bound in China by
South China Printing Company

The publisher would like to thank the following for their kind
permission to reproduce their photographs:
(Key: a=above, b=below/bottom, c=center, l=left, r=right, t=top)
4–5 Corbis: Lewis Mulatero/Galeries (t). **12–13 Corbis:** Lewis
Mulatero/Galeries (t). **13 123RF.com:** Surya Zaidan (br).
19 Corbis: Scubazoo/ SuperStock (br). **20–21 Corbis:** Lewis Mulatero/
Galeries (t). **23 123RF.com:** Surya Zaidan (tr). **28–29 Corbis:** Lewis
Mulatero/Galeries (t). **29 Dreamstime.com:** Stefan Pircher (br).
35 Dorling Kindersley: Jeremy Hunt – modelmaker (tr).
36–37 Corbis: Lewis Mulatero/Galeries (t). **44–45 Getty
Images:** Image Source (t). **45 123RF.com:** Surya Zaidan (br).
Corbis: Stuart Westmorland/Science Faction (br/tiger shark).
Jacket images: Front: Getty Images: Todd Bretl Photography/Flickr Open

All other images © Dorling Kindersley
For further information see: www.dkimages.com

Discover more at
www.dk.com

Contents

Shark Reef

Written by Niki Foreman

The reef sharks

Just beneath the ocean waves, a colorful coral reef bubbled with life. A school of bright blue surgeonfish swam by. The orange-and-white stripes of a clownfish disappeared into a spiky anemone [a-NE-mo-nee]. A sea slug slithered along the ocean floor. A lobster scuttled by. It stopped.

A pair of eyes looked out from an underwater cave. They were locked on the lobster. In a flurry of bubbles and teeth, the lobster was gone. The long, slender body of a young, whitetip reef shark swam away.

Blanche, the whitetip reef shark, was looking for food in the coral reef. She was a shark on a mission. Nothing got in her way once she spied something she wanted.

Over there! An octopus! Blanche plunged after it between the coral.

She almost had it, but something was
behind her. She spun around, and
the octopus vanished into a deep crack.

"You!" Blanche snapped. It was
Ash, the gray reef shark. "You made
me lose my dinner!"

"Ooh, what was it?" Ash asked.

"It was mine!" shouted Blanche.

"I wouldn't be so sure about that!" a voice spoke. "I like a bit of octopus myself."

A large shark with a hammer-shaped head appeared out of nowhere. It circled the coral. The beady eyes on each side of its hammer head watched for any sign of the octopus.

"I'm Harry. Pleased to meet you both!" the stranger said.

Ash stared. "What happened to your head?" he asked.

"My head's special," Harry explained. "It gives me 360-degree vision, which means I can see everything."

"Not quite everything,"
something nearby said. Suddenly,
the coral on the seafloor moved.
Except it wasn't coral; it was a fish!

"Oh! Hi, Moby," said Blanche.
"We didn't see you there!"

"Well, that is the point," Moby
said grumpily. His long beard
of tassels quivered like anemone
tentacles. "I'm camouflaged
on the reef floor!"

"Moby, meet Harry," said Blanche. "Harry, this is Moby. Moby is a wobbegong."

"What kind of fish is a wobbegong?" asked Harry.

"A shark, just like you!" Moby replied, and smiled a big, toothy grin to prove it.

Killer bite

A large shape loomed in the deep ocean.

"Hey! What's that out there?" Ash wondered.

"Let's take a closer look," suggested Harry.

Ash, Blanche, Harry, and Moby swam to the reef's edge— the drop-off—where the seafloor plunged down into the deep sea.

The large shape swam near
the surface, through the shards
of light from the sun's rays.
The creature's gaping mouth
was open wide. Water rushed
into the vast darkness inside.

"It's a whale shark!"
gasped Moby.

Types of shark
There are about 375 species
of shark, which can be
sorted by their features,
such as the number of
gill slits and fins, and
mouth position.

"So, is it a whale, or is it a shark?" asked Blanche.

"It's a shark," answered Moby, "and it's the biggest fish in the ocean! It swims around with its mouth open wide and filters the water for tiny plankton and krill."

"But why?" asked Ash.

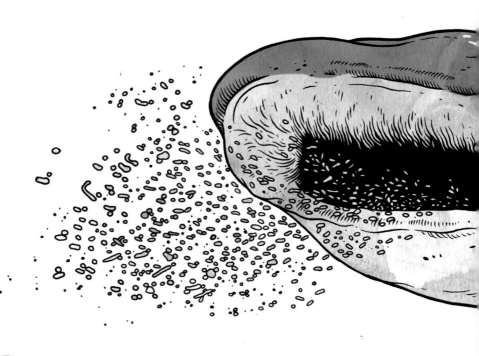

"Because that's what it eats!"
Moby replied.

"But how can a huge fish like
that survive on teeny-tiny plankton?"
wondered Harry.

"Because it eats whale-loads
of them!" explained Moby.

Ash started swimming around with his mouth open wide.

"Ash, what are you doing?" Blanche asked.

"I thought I'd try the whale shark's trick," Ash replied. "See if food will swim into my mouth…"

Blanche rolled her eyes.

"But don't you love the hunt?" she asked. "We're made to hunt. Look at me! I have a blunt snout, protective eye flaps, and tough skin to bash through all that coral without getting hurt—not to mention my sharp teeth for a killer bite. Nothing can get in my way!"

"Except me," Ash laughed.

"I love the hunt, too!" Harry burst out. "My favorite meal is stingray. They hide on the seafloor. In my nose are tiny sensors that can feel any movement from other fish, even if I can't see them. So when I sense a hiding stingray, I use my hammer head to pin it down and then bite off its wings!"

"I have those same sensors in my nose!" Ash exclaimed. "I love hunting with my buddies. We corner schools of snapper against the reef wall. That way, they have nowhere to escape, and then we charge in and feast!"

"That all sounds like far too much effort to me," Moby said. "My clever markings and tassels allow me to stay unseen on the seafloor amongst the coral. Fish come up to me all the time and don't have a clue I'm there!" Moby chuckled.

"So when a fish gets close, that's when I strike! I suck it into my mouth, and eat it alive using my sharp, fanglike teeth. But enough talk about food. I'm getting hungry just thinking about it!" he grumbled.

Sensory pores
Sharks have an extra sense. On their snouts, they have pores that pick up the weak electrical signals that all living things give out—even if they are hiding in the sandy seabed.

Speedy swimmer

A blur of fins, tail, and teeth sped toward the four sharks. It appeared out of nowhere!

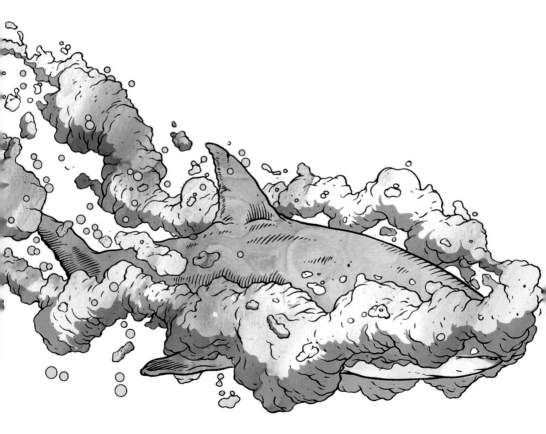

"Howdy, guys!" the blur said, swimming back and forth. "Fin's the name, and speed's the game. I'm a shortfin mako, the fastest shark in these here waters—in any waters, actually! Do you guys live here? I stay on the move myself. All through the great blue, I swim and swim and swim."

Ash gaped in awe at the chatty visitor. "You've really been out there... in the deep ocean?" he asked.

"Sure have!" Fin talked as fast as he swam! He checked the four reef sharks with his large, round eyes. His mouth was set into a grin, and long, curvy teeth stuck out every which way.

"You should see the things I've seen. There's some weird stuff out there! There are small sharks with see-through skin that bite cookie-shaped holes into their prey. There are fish that fish for other fish with bait that looks like tasty food. There are squid that talk to each other. They light up the water with amazing displays, but I'm still learning squid speak!"

Sounds, sight, and smells

Sharks have excellent sight, even in dim light, and some see in color, too. They can pick up sounds and smells that are nearly a mile (1.6 km) away. By moving their heads, they can find the direction they are coming from.

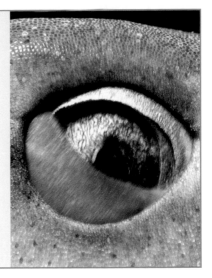

23

"Fin, will you stay still?" Blanche cried out. "You're making me dizzy!"

"No can do, lady," Fin replied. "If I stop swimming, I die! You see, I have weak gills. So if I stop moving, not enough water passes through my gills and I stop breathing, which means lights-out for Fin!"

"But don't you ever get tired?" asked Harry.

"Never! I'm not the fastest shark in the sea for nothing!"

"You're really the fastest shark?" asked Ash. "Prove it!"

"Sure thing," said Fin. "Let's have a race!"

Fin set up a racetrack around the reef. The sharks lined up on the starting line, raring to go.

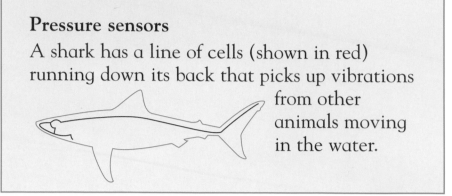

Pressure sensors

A shark has a line of cells (shown in red) running down its back that picks up vibrations from other animals moving in the water.

A ballooned blowfish released a shot of bubbles, and the race was on! Fin was quick off the starting line. The others were hot on his tail around the lagoon and through the turtle nursery. But then Fin sped away and through the seaweed finish line.

"Victory is mine!" he shouted, but didn't stop…

The others crossed the finish line, but Fin was just a speck in the distant blue.

Diving encounter

"Well, I think that's enough excitement for one day," Moby said.

The four sharks turned on their tails and swam back to the shallow waters of the reef.

All of a sudden, Harry's nose sensors started twitching as vibrations from a loud noise hit them. A large speedboat zoomed past overhead. It stopped right above Moby's favorite resting spot. Six divers plunged into the water.

"Typical!" Moby moaned. "Just when I wanted a little bit of peace, more visitors!"

"What are they?" wondered Ash, staring at the visitors.

A survivor!
The Australian Rodney Fox was attacked by a great white shark while competing in a spearfishing competition. After recovering, he built the first shark cage so divers could study sharks.

"Whatever they are, they can stay over there," Blanche said. "I'll mind my own business if they mind theirs!"

Just then, the divers started swimming deeper into the reef, closer to the sharks. Ash hunched into an S-shape.

"Ash! What are you doing?" asked Harry.

"They're making me nervous!" explained Ash. "This is my warning display. If they come any closer, those creatures might get hurt."

"It's not working, Ash. They're getting closer!" said Harry.

31

"Don't worry, guys," Blanche soothed. "Look how weak and slow they are. If they attack, we'll out-swim them easily."

"And look at their mouths," said Moby. "There are no sharp gnashers in there to worry about. They should be scared of us!"

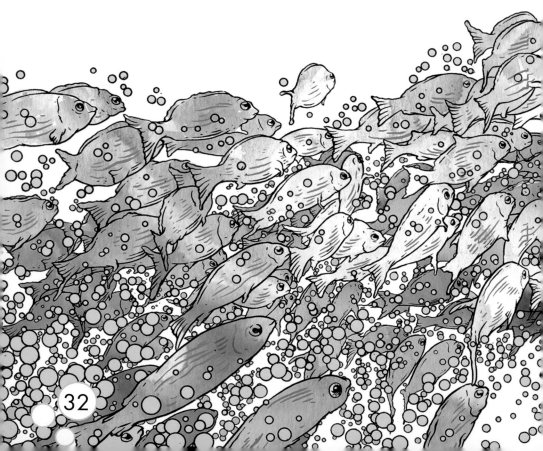

The divers and the sharks
hovered in the water, watching
each other's every move. A diver
pointed at something, but the sudden
movement surprised Ash. He panicked
and swam into the group of divers.
Then he saw what the diver was
pointing at…

"Snapper!" Ash shouted.
His powerful tail propelled him into the large school. The silvery snapper panicked under attack. Ash was excited. "One snapper, two snapper, three snapper…" he counted as he ate greedily.

"He's not having all those to himself!" exclaimed Blanche, and she followed him into the fishy fold. All the bubbles, blood, and noise attracted other sharks from the reef. They appeared from every direction. It was a feeding frenzy!

But wait! What was that noise?

The motorboat had started up again. The latest visitors were leaving the reef.

Designed for hunting

A shark likes to whip around its prey and look for angles from which to attack. Its tail, or caudal fin, provides the driving force. Frenzied movements gain its attention.

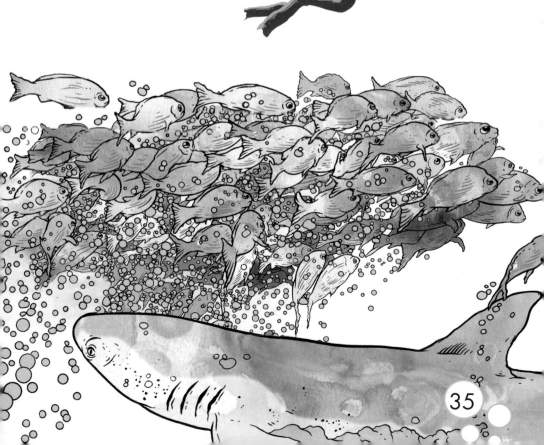

Deadly predator

Sharks and snapper scattered
as the boat sped away. A lonely
flipper drifted down, down, down.
Ash and Blanche followed it.
It landed on the coral—except it
wasn't coral; it was Moby!

"Can't a wobbegong get
a moment's peace?!" Moby shouted.
Ash watched the boat disappear
in the distance. "I'm glad they're
gone. They made me nervous."

Moby chuckled, "I think you
made them nervous. You guys…"

Moby cut off as he looked out to the drop-off. What was there made the four sharks freeze in terror.

A hefty shark powered toward the reef. Blanche, Ash, Harry, and Moby caught sight of the tell-tale stripes on its back.

"Tiger shark!" whispered Blanche. She was shaking with fear. "I've heard that tiger sharks eat whitetip reef sharks," she said.

"Stay absolutely still," replied Moby. "Let's not find out…"

"I heard about one brave whitetip who stood up to a tiger shark once," said Harry.

"Really?" Blanche asked in hope. "What happened?"

"The whitetip was never seen again," he replied.

Blanche gulped.

Deadly bite

A shark's mouth has powerful jaws and rows of razor-sharp teeth. Its tastebuds are on its mouth, and not on its small, thick tongue. Sharks can be fussy eaters, spitting out prey that they don't like.

The tiger shark suddenly spun its massive bulk around. Its wide snout housed a set of formidable jaws. Its powerful tail propelled it through the water. It was heading straight for them.

Suddenly, it halted, and in a dreadful coughing fit, it coughed up its entire stomach! The stomach floated in the water. Stomach juices and its last dinner seeped out.

A rubber tire bobbed among
the stomach juices.

Once it was empty, the stomach
was gulped back down. Hungry
again, the tiger shark rushed to
the surface, gobbled up an albatross
and landed back in the water with
a deafening **CRASH!**

The four sharks breathed
a sigh of relief as the tiger shark
swam away from the reef.
They stared at the rubber tire.

"What is it?" asked Ash.

"It could be anything,"
Moby replied. "Tiger sharks are
scavengers. They prowl the ocean
and eat whatever they come across,
whether it's edible or not!"

As the sun set, four unlikely friends swam through the coral reef.

"I hope we have more visitors tomorrow!" said Ash.

"I hope we don't!" Blanche frowned, before plunging between the coral. An octopus tentacle retreated into a deep crack, just in time.

The big three

The big three predators to look out for!

GREAT WHITE   BULL SHARK   TIGER SHARK

Bull shark
This aggressive shark can be found not only in tropical waters along shores, but also swimming inland along freshwater rivers.

Great white shark
At the top of the food chain, this 21-ft- (6.5-m-) long ferocious hunter is a threat to any large fish and sea mammal.

Tiger shark
This savage scavenger is not a fussy eater and will swallow anything, even garbage drifting in the ocean.

Glossary

Anemone
Sea animal with
a baglike body and
stinging tentacles.

Coral
Soft and hard animals
that stay fixed in
one place and live
together in colonies.

Food chain
A diagram that
shows what foods
animals eat.

Frenzy
An act of
uncontrolled and
wild excitement.

Freshwater
Water that doesn't
contain the salt
found in the sea.

Gills
Opening on a fish's
head that supplies
oxygen in the water
to the fish's eye
and brain.

Gnashers
Another name
for teeth.

Lagoon
Shallow pondlike
water between
shore and reef.

Nursery
Area for babies.

Plankton
Tiny plants and
animals that
drift in water.

Predator
Animal that
hunts another.

Reef
A ridge of rock,
coral, or sand
just below the
ocean's surface.

Scavenger
An animal that
eats dead animals.

School
Large group of fish
that swim together.

Sea grass
Leafy plants that can
flower under water
and provide food and
water for sea animals.

Sensors
Way of receiving
signals.

Species
A type of animal.

Tentacle
Long arm of a sea
animal used to
catch food.

Tropical
Found in the
tropics—an area
with a hot and sticky
(humid) climate.

Vibration
A shaking movement.

Index

DK READERS help children learn to read, then read to learn. If you enjoyed this DK READER, then look out for these other titles for your child.

Level 3 African Adventure
Experience the trip of a lifetime on an African safari as recorded in Katie's diary. Share her excitement at seeing wild animals up close.

Level 3 Rain Forest Explorer
Through her blog, Zoe shares the thrill and narrow escapes as she travels through the Amazon rain forest to her Uncle's Research Station. What will she discover?

Level 3 LEGO® Friends: Summer Adventures
Enjoy a summer of fun in Heartlake City with Emma, Mia, Andrea, Stephanie, Olivia, and friends.